MARTIN *Van Buren*

MARTIN *Van Buren*

OUR EIGHTH PRESIDENT

By Steven Ferry

SPIRIT
of America™

The Child's World®, Inc.
Chanhassen, Minnesota

8

MARTIN *Van Buren*

Published in the United States of America by The Child's World®, Inc.
PO Box 326 • Chanhassen, MN 55317-0326 • 800-599-READ • www.childsworld.com

Acknowledgments
The Creative Spark: Mary Francis-DeMarois, Project Director; Elizabeth Sirimarco Budd, Series Editor; Robert Court, Design and Art Direction; Janine Graham, Page Layout; Jennifer Moyers, Production

The Child's World®, Inc.: Mary Berendes, Publishing Director; Red Line Editorial, Fact Research; Cindy Klingel, Curriculum Advisor; Robert Noyed, Historical Advisor

Photos
Cover: White House Collection, courtesy White House Historical Association; Bettmann/Corbis: 8, 12, 17, 22, 23; ©Lee Snider/Corbis: 34; Frances G. Mayer/Corbis: 6; Independence National Historical Park: 9, Library of Congress Collections: 14, 17, 20, 21, 29, 30, 32, 33, 35; Courtesy of the National Museum of the American Indian, Smithsonian Institution: 27; Historical Picture Archive/Corbis: 11; Stock Montage: 7, 10, 13, 25, 26; Woolaroc Museum, Bartlesville, Oklahoma: 28

Registration
The Child's World®, Inc., Spirit of America™, and their associated logos are the sole property and registered trademarks of The Child's World®, Inc.

Library of Congress Cataloging-in-Publication Data
Ferry, Steven, 1953–
    Martin Van Buren : our eighth president / by Steven Ferry.
        p. cm.
    ISBN 1-56766-837-2 (alk. paper)
    1. Van Buren, Martin, 1782–1862-Juvenile literature. 2. Presidents—United States—Biography—Juvenile literature. [1. Van Buren, Martin, 1782–1862. 2. Presidents.]   I. Title.
    E387 .F47 2001
    973.5'7'092—dc21
                                                    00-010602

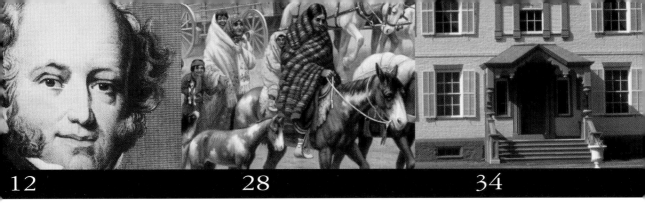

12   28   34

Contents

Chapter ONE

The Young Politician

Martin Van Buren rose from a simple life in a small town to win the nation's highest public office. He became the eighth president in 1837 after years of important government positions.

IN 1782, THE UNITED STATES HAD JUST WON the Revolutionary War and was entering an exciting time in its history. That same year, future president Martin Van Buren was born on December 5 in Kinderhook, New York. He was the third of Abraham and Maria Van Buren's eight children. Their family had farmed in the Hudson Valley for 150 years before Abraham Van Buren turned their farmhouse into a tavern. He was also involved in Kinderhook's government. The town often used his tavern as a **polling place** for state and national elections.

At that time, Kinderhook was the center of life between the cities of Albany and Poughkeepsie. It was also a stopping point for those traveling from New York City to Albany.

Many lawyers and politicians visited the tavern to drink and discuss **politics.** Abraham Van Buren supported Thomas Jefferson's **political party,** the Democratic-Republicans, but he was careful to remain **neutral** in these discussions. He did not want to have disagreements with his customers.

Van Buren was born in this house in Kinderhook. His family had owned and farmed the surrounding land for more than 150 years.

Little Mat, as people called Martin, had a job from a young age. He pulled a heavy sled of groceries through the snow, making deliveries to people around town. Afterward, he would rush home to help at the family tavern. There he would listen carefully to the

7

Kinderhook sat in the beautiful Hudson Valley in upstate New York. Dutch farmers inhabited much of the region. In fact, many people in the area—including the Van Burens—spoke Dutch as well as English.

discussions, noting how his father always listened but said little. His father believed in Thomas Jefferson's **principles** of a limited national government. Jefferson believed the states should have more power than the **federal** government. Little Mat learned about these ideas during those long nights at the tavern.

Little Mat studied in the poorly lit village schoolhouse and then briefly at the Kinderhook Academy. The schoolmaster was impressed with Mat's ability to read and write, but he left school before he was 14 years old. He planned to work as an **apprentice** under a local attorney from 1796 until 1802. For the first year, Mat cleaned the office and copied **documents** by hand. He had more responsibilities by the time he was 15. In fact, he was already arguing his first case in front of a jury. Within a few short years, Martin Van Buren was ready for a change. He was interested in politics. So at age 18, he began working to help Thomas Jefferson win the presidential election of 1800.

Leaders in the Democratic-Republican Party noticed young Van Buren. He was elected to the congressional **caucus** in Troy. Meanwhile, he continued his career as a lawyer, working for William P. Van Ness and finishing his law studies in 1803. Then Van Buren returned to Kinderhook to practice law. He became one of the best-known lawyers in New York by defending the small farmers and shopkeepers of the area against rich landowners.

Shortly after opening his own law practice, Van Buren married his childhood sweetheart, Hannah Hoes. Hannah was a distant cousin of the same age. They wed on February 21, 1807, as soon as Van Buren felt he could support a family.

The Van Burens admired the ideas of Thomas Jefferson, the leader of the Democratic-Republican Party. Jefferson believed in a true democracy, a country that would place power in the hands of its citizens. His principles would guide Van Buren's political life for years to come.

9

Martin Van Buren and Hannah Hoes grew up together in Kinderhook. The childhood sweethearts married in 1807, but theirs would be a short marriage. Hannah died just 12 years later.

Interesting Facts

▸ Kinderhook was the model for the town in *The Legend of Sleepy Hollow,* the famous story by Washington Irving about the Headless Horseman. In fact, Irving wrote the story while staying at the Van Buren's home.

Their marriage was a happy one, and Hannah was a loving and gentle person. They had six sons before she died on February 5, 1819. Four of the children survived. Both of Van Buren's parents had died shortly before Hannah, so this was a sad time in his life. Van Buren never married again.

The name "Little Mat" stuck with Van Buren because he never grew taller than 5 feet, 6 inches. He was known in later years as "Little Van." He held himself upright and always dressed very neatly in fine clothing. Whenever he could get away from his duties, he liked to fish or attend plays and operas. The twinkle in his eye, his cheerful optimism, and his quick, enthusiastic conversation made him popular.

Van Buren may have been good at conversation, but he learned from his father to let others do the talking when it came to political subjects. Van Buren rarely took sides. Over the years, he developed a reputation for being **evasive** and shrewd. He had great **ambition,** but he also stuck by his principles, even when they made him unpopular.

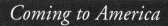

CORNELIS VAN BUURMALSEN WAS A YOUNG FARMER LIVING NEAR AMSTERDAM, the capital of the Netherlands. In 1631, he signed a contract with a man who owned land in the New Netherlands (modern-day New York State). In the contract, Cornelis promised to farm the man's land in the New Netherlands for three years for about $92 in pay. In exchange, he received free transport to America.

After the three years, Cornelis returned to Amsterdam and signed another contract. This time, he received his own land to farm. He sailed back to America with his new wife and their son, who was born on the long ocean journey. They landed at New Amsterdam on March 4, 1637, exactly 200 years before their great-great-great-grandson, Martin Van Buren, became the eighth president of the United States on March 4, 1837.

Cornelis was a good farmer. On October 24, 1646, he bought a large farm in Manhattan. His farm was located in what is today the bustling part of New York City called Greenwich Village. Their second son bought land at Kinderhook, which was to become the family home where Martin Van Buren grew up.

Chapter TWO

The Red Fox of Kinderhook

As a lawyer in his home-town, Van Buren took his first steps toward an important political career.

WHILE STILL PRACTICING LAW AND RAISING his family, Van Buren began to pursue a political career. In 1809, he was named the chairman of the Democratic-Republican meetings in Albany, the New York State capital. By 1812, he had been elected to the state senate. He held the position until 1820.

It was common at the time to put people in jail if they owed money but could not pay it back. Van Buren worked to end this practice. He also supported the War of 1812 against Great Britain. The British navy had been stopping U.S. ships and kidnap-ping American sailors. U.S. military forces needed more men. Van Buren proposed a **bill** to **draft** men into the American army and navy.

The Democratic-Republican Party in New York was split into two groups: the followers of New York Governor DeWitt Clinton, and their rivals, the Bucktails. Van Buren became the leader of the Bucktails. This group helped him become the state attorney general in 1816. As the attorney general, Van Buren was the most important lawyer in the state of New York.

Because life was difficult on British navy ships, some sailors would run away when they arrived in American ports. The British navy began to attack U.S. ships and kidnap the British sailors, as well as some American sailors. This was one cause of the War of 1812, which Van Buren firmly supported.

13

During his career, Martin Van Buren had many nicknames. His critics compared him to various animals, such as a fox and, in this cartoon, an opossum. These comparisons suggested that Van Buren was sneaky and refused to tell people what he really thought. Here, the "opossum" carries other politicians in his pouch.

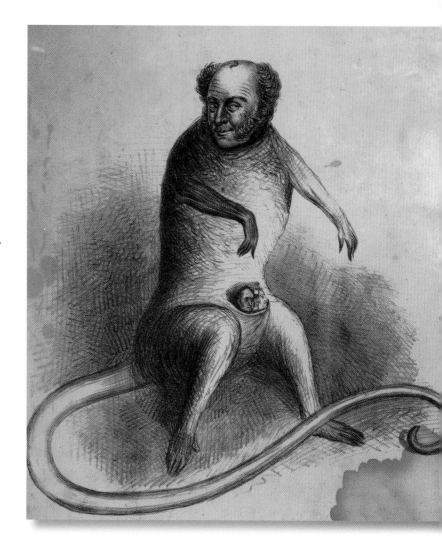

Governor Clinton removed him from this position three years later. Van Buren and the Bucktail Party decided to challenge the governor. They formed a powerful group called the Albany Regency. These politicians won votes by using their power to help people who voted for them. During this time, people began to call Van Buren "The Little Magician" and "The Red Fox of Kinderhook." These names were given to him because of the sly, crafty way in which he achieved his goals.

Van Buren's success in politics continued. In 1821, he was elected to the U.S. Senate. He immediately began working to reform voting laws. At that time, most states had rules about who could vote. Usually, only white men who owned land and paid taxes were allowed to cast ballots. Van Buren believed that all white men should be given the right to vote.

The next year, Van Buren suggested that Florida be admitted to the **Union,** which is another name for the United States. But there was a problem. Many people in Florida kept slaves. The northerners didn't want another slave state in the Union, but the southerners did. Van Buren came up with a way to give both sides part of what they wanted. He suggested that slave owners could keep any slaves who were already in Florida, but no new slaves could be brought into the **territory.** It would be another two decades before Florida became a state, but politicians on both sides of the slavery issue liked Van Buren's ideas.

Van Buren continued to follow the principles of Thomas Jefferson as he took action in the Senate. Like Jefferson, Van Buren did not want a strong central government. He believed instead that the states should have more power. Like George Washington, Van Buren believed the United States should remain neutral in disputes between other countries. In 1826, President John Quincy Adams planned to send an American **representative** to the Panama Congress. This meeting would set up a united force of countries that would fight together against other unfriendly countries. When the president proposed this to the Senate, Van Buren spoke out against U.S. attendance at the Congress. He believed it went against America's policy of staying neutral.

Van Buren also united the Democratic-Republicans in the various states. By so doing, he helped found the Democratic Party that is still a force in American politics. Van Buren was one of the first politicians to understand how to use political parties. He realized that political success depended on using the newspapers and large meetings to spread the party's

ideas to the many new voters in the country. He also realized that members of a party had to be well organized and loyal. "Political parties are inseparable from free government," Van Buren once said, "and are highly useful to the country." He believed that a strong, honest political party could keep one individual from abusing power.

In 1828, Andrew Jackson was the Democratic Party's presidential **candidate.**

By 1824, most states allowed all white men to vote. The number of voters greatly increased over the next two decades. In this picture, a crowd of men gathers to vote in a local tavern, much as they did at the Van Buren family's tavern in Kinderhook.

War hero Andrew Jackson lost the presidential election of 1824 to John Quincy Adams, but he was very popular with the American people. Four years later, Van Buren helped expand Jackson's image as a leader for working-class Americans. Jackson won a great majority of votes in the election of 1828, when more Americans cast their ballots than ever before.

Jackson was a war hero from the South. Van Buren supported Jackson and worked hard to help him win the presidency. To accomplish this, Van Buren helped create an image of Andrew Jackson as someone who cared about the common people. Van Buren also had a plan to get the votes of more powerful Americans. He continued to control politics in New York State through the Albany Regency. Van Buren used the Regency to help himself get elected governor of New York. This gave Van Buren the power to win the state's 36 electoral votes for Jackson.

Less than three months later, Van Buren resigned as governor when President Jackson offered him a post in his **cabinet.** Even in his short term as governor, Van Buren managed to accomplish something important.

He sponsored the Safety Fund Plan, which forced New York banks to set up a special fund to protect their customers. At that time, people lost all their savings if a bank went out of business. The money in this fund would be used to repay customers if a bank failed.

When Van Buren accepted the position in Jackson's cabinet in 1829, he became the secretary of state. This meant he was in charge of U.S. relations with other countries. In 1830, Van Buren signed two **treaties.** The first was with Turkey. It allowed the United States to sail the Black Sea. The second treaty was with Great Britain. It renewed trade with British territories in the West Indies.

In 1832, it was time for another presidential election. The Democratic Party again chose Jackson as its candidate. Then Van Buren received the **nomination** for vice president. During the **campaign,** Jackson and Van Buren promised to provide more opportunities for the common man. They won the election on December 5. Over the next four years, Van Buren supported Jackson on almost everything.

This portrait of Van Buren was painted during his brief time as governor of New York. The capitol building in Albany is visible in the background. Van Buren left his position as governor after just a few months when he became a member of Jackson's cabinet.

Jackson set up Van Buren to be the next president. Van Buren easily won the Democratic presidential nomination in 1836. The opposition, the Whig Party, had three candidates running in the election. Van Buren received the most electoral votes, far more than all his opponents combined.

20

AS A MEMBER OF JACKSON'S cabinet, Van Buren became the president's closest advisor. Other members of the cabinet grew jealous. They accused Van Buren of being sneaky and untrustworthy, but Jackson described him as "a true man."

Peggy Eaton was the new wife of the secretary of war, John Eaton. The other cabinet members and their wives treated Mrs. Eaton badly. They believed she was immoral. Rumors spread that she had lived with John Eaton before they were married. Jackson and Van Buren defended Mrs. Eaton, and tensions grew within the cabinet.

In the spring of 1831, Van Buren came up with an idea. If he and John Eaton resigned from their posts, Jackson could ask all the other cabinet members to leave, too. Jackson agreed with the plan. This political cartoon depicts the members of Jackson's cabinet (including Van Buren, second from right) as rats that are scurrying away from the president.

Jackson appointed a new cabinet, and he rewarded Van Buren by naming him **minister** to Great Britain. The position did not last long, however. He returned to the United States in 1832 to run for the vice presidency.

21

Chapter THREE

The Careful Dutchman

Some people called Van Buren "The Careful Dutchman" because he never made quick decisions. This careful approach to leadership did not help Van Buren during his difficult presidency. Little did he know when he first took office that the country was about to enter a depression.

JACKSON'S POPULARITY HAD HELPED VAN BUREN win the election of 1836. At his **inauguration** in 1837, Van Buren promised to "tread in the footsteps" of the great President Jackson. He also talked about the country's good fortune. He discussed how the "American experiment" with democracy was setting an example for the rest of the world to follow.

Just a few weeks later, however, the Panic of 1837 set in. The money problems of the time set the pace for Van Buren's presidency. In fact, the nation entered the worst **depression** it had experienced up to that time. Van Buren was unable to solve this problem.

The trouble started when President Jackson took the government's money out of the Second Bank of the United States, which

was the national bank at the time. Then he placed the money in smaller state banks. These banks unwisely loaned money to people who wanted to buy land in the West. The people bought the land with the money they borrowed, hoping it would increase in value. If it did, they could sell the land for a profit and pay back their loans. This plan was risky. A great deal of land actually became less valuable in 1837, but the people still had to pay back their loans. Unfortunately, they had no money to do this, which forced many banks to close.

At his inauguration, Van Buren promised that the country would continue to enjoy the good financial times of Jackson's presidency. Unfortunately, the Panic of 1837 started almost immediately after he took office.

Interesting Facts

▸ One of Van Buren's many nicknames was "The Little Magician," referring to his small size and his cleverness. "It is said that he is a great magician," President Jackson once said. "I believe it, but his only wand is good common sense which he uses for the benefit of the country."

▸ Another nickname that people called Van Buren was "Martin Van Ruin" because of the long depression during his presidency.

Jackson tried to stop this abuse during his last months in office. He ordered that land be purchased only with gold or silver. Americans rushed to the banks to exchange their paper money for these precious metals. Unfortunately, the banks simply didn't have enough gold and silver to supply the demand. At the same time, three English banks failed. The remaining English banks wanted back any money they had loaned to American banks.

With no real money left, banks in Philadelphia and New York City closed on May 10, 1837, and the panic began. Hundreds of other banks and businesses failed. Thousands of people lost their homes, their land, and their jobs. Most of the factories on the East Coast closed. In some cities, people rioted for food. Eventually, nearly 1,000 banks around the country failed. At the same time, Van Buren wore expensive clothes. He drove around the streets of Washington in a luxurious horse-drawn coach driven by men in fancy uniforms. This made him unpopular with Americans, who thought he was behaving more like a king than a U.S. president.

Van Buren continued Jackson's policies. He also worked to establish an independent **treasury** to deal with U.S. government money. He did not want state banks or another national bank looking after it. The treasury would make sure the national government did not spend more money than it had.

Many congressmen didn't like this idea because it would take money from banks in their home states. It was not until Van Buren's final year in office that Congress approved the treasury. Unfortunately, the depression had hurt many Americans. Some even starved or froze to death. Van Buren did nothing to help because he did not feel it was the government's job to help individuals. "The less government interferes with private pursuits the better," Van Buren said. His failure to handle the crisis lost him his popularity and the next election.

Van Buren's handling of Native Americans was not much better. In 1835, the government tried to force the Seminole Indians to move

Van Buren moved into the White House as a widower with four unmarried sons. Without a first lady, he had no one to act as a hostess. About 18 months after his inauguration, Van Buren's eldest son, Abraham, married Angelica Singleton (above). Abraham served as Van Buren's private secretary, and Angelica acted as the hostess at White House parties.

West, and the Second Seminole War began. This war was not popular with Americans. Over six years, it cost $20 million that could have been spent in better ways. The public also didn't like the way the leader, Chief Osceola, was unfairly captured during a **truce.**

In 1838, Van Buren could have stopped the forced removal of 18,000 Cherokees, mostly from Georgia, to **reservations** west of the Mississippi. The Supreme Court said that the Native Americans had the right to remain on their lands, and most Americans did not support the removal. But Van Buren would not cancel Jackson's 1830 Indian Removal Act. Four thousand Cherokees died of cold, hunger, and disease on what became known as "The Trail of Tears."

While Van Buren was slow to deal with problems at home, he did slightly better

In 1839, the Spanish ship Amistad *was transporting African slaves. The slaves suddenly seized the ship, hoping to win their freedom. They sailed the ship to Connecticut, and American leaders had to decide what to do with them. Van Buren ordered that they be returned to the Spanish. This angered many Americans who were against slavery. Finally, a U.S. federal court decided to help the slaves. It ordered that they be freed and returned to their homeland.*

handling those with other countries. In 1837, the British controlled Canada. A group of Canadian rebels attacked British soldiers there. The attack failed, and the rebels escaped to an island in the Niagara River. Some Americans began to help the rebels. They sent supplies to them on the steamship *Caroline.* In December, Canadian troops working for the British captured the *Caroline* and set it on fire, killing an American.

During Van Buren's term, the United States took over vast expanses of Native American lands. Americans did not always like the tactics the army used. Some were angered when soldiers captured the fearless warrior Chief Osceola (above) after the United States and his tribe had called a truce.

Van Buren was angered by the attack, but he was also unhappy that Americans had ignored the U.S. policy of remaining neutral. He believed the Americans should not have helped the Canadian rebels. Although Congress wanted him to declare war on Britain, Van Buren refused. He insisted that America must remain neutral. He sent an army to the

Van Buren continued to enforce Jackson's Indian Removal Act during his own presidency. As a result, 18,000 Cherokees were forced to leave their homes and sacred lands. In the winter of 1838–1839, they walked or rode about 1,000 miles into what is now the state of Oklahoma.

Canadian border, hoping to calm the situation and avoid war. The rebels gave up on January 13.

The following year, fighting broke out between Canada and America in what became known as the Aroostook War. Lumberjacks from Maine and New Brunswick fought over who owned the trees in the Aroostook Valley. Van Buren continued his policy of neutrality. He sent General Winfield Scott to stop the fighting and negotiate a peace treaty, which was signed on March 25, 1839.

28

IN 1816, A **CHARTER** gave the Second Bank of the United States the right to handle the country's money for the next 20 years. This bank was not run by the government, but was owned by 200 of the richest men in America and some foreigners. The bank had the power from Congress to print money whenever it wanted. It controlled how much money was available. This gave the bank great power over the United States government and its citizens. In 1836, the bank's charter would expire. That meant Congress had to decide whether to keep the Second Bank open. The bank's president, Nicholas Biddle, paid many congressmen, businessmen, and members of the press so they would help keep the bank in business.

Jackson and Van Buren fought for the common man. They believed the bank only helped the rich, and thought that it should help all Americans instead. The cartoon above shows them fighting a "many-headed monster." It represents Biddle, the Second Bank, and the people who supported it. In 1833, Jackson took the government's money out of the Second Bank. Unfortunately, this led to the Panic of 1837. But Van Buren and Jackson finally had their way when the bank was closed in 1836.

Chapter FOUR

Standing Firm

This photo of Van Buren was taken around the time of his last campaign for the presidency in 1848.

VAN BUREN LOST HIS POPULARITY OVER THE four years of his term because of the depression and other problems, such as the Trail of Tears and the Seminole War. Nonetheless, the Democrats still nominated him for the presidential election of 1840. The election became known as the "hard cider campaign." Van Buren's opponents, the Whigs, insisted that he was so much like a king, he would rather drink French wine than American cider.

The Whigs paraded their candidate, William Henry Harrison, around the country with music and free cider for people to drink. They claimed that Harrison was a man of the people. He won the election with 234 electoral votes to Van Buren's 60. Van Buren had been beaten by the same techniques he had

invented to get Jackson elected president—promoting a candidate who would appeal to the common man. "Van, Van, is a used up man," the Whigs chanted.

Van Buren ran twice more for president, but he failed both times. When he attended the Democratic Party **convention** in 1844, he had the support of the majority of the party. Then he refused to support the **annexation** of Texas. The **Republic** of Texas had gained its independence from Mexico in 1836 and wanted to be accepted into the United States. Even though many Americans approved, Van Buren did not. Allowing Texas into the Union would have added another slave state. It would also have resulted in a war with Mexico. Because Van Buren stood

During his campaign to become president, William Henry Harrison traveled around the country with a small log cabin and hard (alcoholic) cider that he offered to voters. Harrison was a rich man who lived in a mansion, not a log cabin. Still, he described Van Buren as someone who lived like a king and didn't understand the needs of the average American. In truth, Van Buren did care about the common man, but people didn't believe this after listening to Harrison and members of his campaign.

firm to his principles, he lost the nomination. James Polk was nominated instead and went on to become president, annexing Texas and spreading slavery in the Union.

By the next presidential election, Van Buren had become even more opposed to slavery. He was nominated as a candidate for president in 1848 by the Free Soil Party. This group was devoted to opposing slavery. Van Buren came in third and retired from politics.

The 1850 census described him as a "farmer," but he was still regarded by many as an **elder statesman.**

In 1852, Van Buren traveled to Europe, where he lived for the next two years. He was the first ex-president to leave the United States. In Italy, he began writing his life story, in which he discussed his lifelong ambition to win "the glittering prize" of the presidency.

Van Buren returned to the United States and settled down. His home, called

This 1848 campaign poster shows Van Buren with his vice presidential candidate, Charles Francis Adams. Mr. Adams was the son of another former president, John Quincy Adams. Van Buren and Adams ran as candidates for the Free Soil Party, which opposed slavery.

Lindenwald, was a large, two-story brick house in Kinderhook. The Van Ness family, friends of the Van Burens, had built the house back in 1797. By 1824, they could no longer afford it. Martin Van Buren paid $14,000 for the house and the surrounding land in 1839. He turned it into a working farm. Over the years, he expanded the house and made it more beautiful. He also installed modern conveniences, such as ranges in the kitchen, running water, a bath, and a water heater.

Van Buren's son John followed in his father's footsteps. He and his father led the Barnburners, a group within the Democratic Party. John Van Buren was also a member of the U.S. Congress from 1841 to 1843.

Although Van Buren never held another public office, he still took an interest in politics. He supported both Franklin Pierce and Abraham Lincoln during their presidential elections.

On July 24, 1862, Van Buren died of asthma. The funeral procession to the cemetery included 81 carriages carrying people who had come to pay their last respects. Van Buren was buried beside his wife and parents.

Each December 5, the day Martin Van Buren was born, a ceremony is held at a local church in honor of a man who set high goals and reached them. Van Buren was an enthusiastic and clever politician. Unfortunately, he was not able to help the country when it truly needed a leader. He is not remembered as the greatest U.S. president, but Martin Van Buren was willing to stand by his principles—even when they made him unpopular.

Lindenwald in Kinderhook was Van Buren's home from 1839 until his death in 1862. With the help of an architect, he remodeled the house into an elegant mansion. The building is now a National Historic Site.

NEW YORK WAS STILL A slave state when Van Buren was born, and his father owned six slaves. Van Buren himself owned a slave, a man named Tom. Van Buren made no effort to find Tom after he ran away in 1814. When Tom was found living in Massachusetts 10 years later, Van Buren agreed to sell him as long as he could be captured "without violence."

While in office, Van Buren tried to find a **compromise** between the southern states, which wanted to keep their slaves, and the northern states, which preferred to end slavery. Only a compromise would keep the Union together, and he found one. He believed the government should let slavery continue where it already existed, but not spread.

In his later years, Van Buren opposed slavery completely. In 1843, he and his son John led the Barnburners, a group within the Democratic Party that was against slavery. Their critics thought they were too unwilling to compromise. They called them "Barnburners" after a farmer who burned down his barn to get rid of the rats. Because the other Democrats would not agree with them about slavery, the Barnburners left the Democratic Party in 1848 and joined the Free Soil Party. On August 9, 1848, the Soilers nominated Van Buren for president. He would not to return to office, however. A southern slave owner and military hero named Zachary Taylor won the election.

1782 Martin Van Buren is born in Kinderhook, New York, on December 5.

1801 Van Buren is elected as a representative to the Democratic-Republican party caucus in Troy, New York. His idol, Thomas Jefferson, becomes president in March. Van Buren avidly supports Jefferson's principles of government for the rest of his life.

1803 Van Buren begins to practice law.

1807 Van Buren marries his cousin and childhood sweetheart, Hannah Hoes, on February 21.

1812 Van Buren is elected state senator. He becomes the leader of the Jeffersonian Democratic-Republicans in New York. During the War of 1812, he proposes a bill to begin drafting men into the military.

1816 Van Buren is named the attorney general of New York.

1819 Hannah Hoes Van Buren dies of tuberculosis. Governor Clinton removes Van Buren from his position as attorney general. To combat the governor, Van Buren and his colleagues establish the Albany Regency, a powerful political group.

1821 Van Buren is elected a U.S. senator.

1826 Van Buren discourages President John Quincy Adams's attempt to send representatives to the Panama Congress, believing that it goes against the nation's policy of neutrality.

1828 Van Buren manages Andrew Jackson's presidential campaign. With the help of the Albany Regency, Van Buren is elected governor of New York.

1829 Van Buren is governor of New York for 71 days before Jackson names him the secretary of state. Throughout Jackson's two terms as president, Van Buren will be his chief advisor.

1831 Van Buren resigns from Jackson's cabinet when other members mistreat Peggy Eaton, wife of Secretary of War John Eaton. He does this so that Jackson can ask other cabinet members for their resignations. Afterward, Jackson names Van Buren minister to Great Britain, an important post.

1832 The Democratic Party nominates Van Buren as Jackson's vice presidential candidate. They win the election in December.

1833 President Jackson pulls government money out of the Second Bank of America and puts it into smaller state banks. This leads to speculation on land in the West and eventually to a severe depression.

1834 The Whig Party is formed to oppose Jackson and Van Buren's Democratic Party.

1836 Jackson orders that land be purchased only with gold or silver, not with paper money. Americans rush to banks to exchange paper money for precious metals. Jackson supports Martin Van Buren as the Democratic presidential candidate. Van Buren is elected the eighth president of the United States by a large number of votes.

1837 The Panic of 1837 begins when banks stop converting paper money to silver and gold. The United States enters a conflict with Canada over the *Caroline* Affair.

1838 Eighteen thousand Cherokees are forced from their homes as part of the Indian Removal Act. Four thousand of them die along the "Trail of Tears." The Aroostook War over the boundary between Maine and Canada begins.

1839 Van Buren orders that the African slaves who had seized the Spanish ship *Amistad* be returned to their Spanish owners. A federal court later decides to help the slaves.

1840 Van Buren signs the Independent Treasury Act, which many consider the major accomplishment of his presidency. William Henry Harrison defeats Van Buren in the presidential election.

1844 Van Buren loses the Democratic presidential nomination to James K. Polk.

1848 Van Buren is the presidential candidate of the Free Soil Party, but Zachary Taylor, a southern slaveholder, is elected. Van Buren retires from political life.

1852 Van Buren travels to Europe, becoming the first president to go abroad after his term.

1862 Van Buren dies at his Lindenwald estate on July 24.

ambition (am-BISH-un)
Ambition is a strong desire to succeed. Van Buren had ambition to do well in politics.

annexation (an-ek-SAY-shun)
Annexation is the joining of something smaller (such as a territory) to something bigger (such as a country). Van Buren was against the annexation of Texas.

apprentice (uh-PREN-tiss)
An apprentice is a person who is learning a skill under the teaching of an expert worker. At age 14, Van Buren worked as an apprentice to an attorney in order to learn about the law.

bill (BILL)
A bill is an idea for a new law that is presented to a group of lawmakers. Van Buren proposed a bill to draft men into the military.

cabinet (KAB-eh-net)
A cabinet is the group of people who advise a president. President Jackson offered Van Buren a position in his cabinet.

campaign (kam-PAYN)
A campaign is the process of running for an election, including activities such as giving speeches or attending rallies. During their campaign, Jackson and Van Buren promised more opportunities to common people.

candidate (KAN-duh-det)
A candidate is a person running in an election. Several candidates run for president every four years.

caucus (KAW-kus)
A caucus is a meeting of a political group to make plans, choose candidates, and decide how to vote. Van Buren attended his first caucus in 1801.

charter (CHAR-tur)
A charter is when the government gives a person or group a special right to do something. In 1816, a charter gave the Second Bank of the United States the right to handle the country's money for the next 20 years.

compromise (KOM-pruh-myz)
A compromise is a way to settle a disagreement in which both sides give up part of what they want. Van Buren tried to keep the country united by making the leaders of the North and the South reach a compromise.

convention (kun-VEN-shun)
A convention is a meeting. Political parties hold national conventions every four years to choose their presidential candidates.

depression (deh-PRESH-un)
A depression is a period of time in which there is little business activity, and many people are out of work. The Panic of 1837 started a depression.

documents (DOK-yuh-ments)
Documents are written or printed papers that give people important information. Van Buren copied documents by hand when he was a lawyer's apprentice.

draft (DRAFT)
When the government drafts people, it makes them join the military as soldiers. Van Buren proposed a bill to draft men into the army and navy.

**elder statesman
(EL-dur STAYTZ-man)**
An elder statesman is an older politician who has left office and is still asked for advice. Van Buren was an elder statesman until he died.

**electoral votes
(ee-LEKT-uh-rul VOHTZ)**
Electoral votes are votes cast by representatives of the American public for the president and vice president. Each state chooses representatives who vote for a candidate in an election. These representatives vote according to what the majority of people in their state want.

evasive (ee-VAY-sive)
If people are evasive, they avoid answering questions about their opinions. Van Buren had a reputation for being evasive.

federal (FED-ur-ul)
Federal means having to do with the central government of the United States, rather than a state or city government. Thomas Jefferson believed the states should have more power than the federal government.

**inauguration
(ih-naw-gyuh-RAY-shun)**
An inauguration is the ceremony
that takes place when a new president
begins a term. Van Buren spoke of
the nation's good fortune at his
inauguration.

minister (MIH-neh-stir)
A minister is a person who is in
charge of one part of the government.
Van Buren was briefly the minister
to Great Britain.

neutral (NOO-trul)
If people are neutral, they do not take
sides. Van Buren believed the United
States should be neutral and not take
sides in problems that arose among
other nations.

nomination (nom-uh-NAY-shun)
If someone receives a nomination,
he or she is chosen by a political
party to run for an office, such as
the presidency. Van Buren received
the Democratic nomination for
vice president.

**political party
(puh-LIT-uh-kul PAR-tee)**
A political party is a group of people
who share similar ideas about how to
run a government. Martin Van Buren
helped found the Democratic Party
of today.

politics (PAWL-uh-tiks)
Politics refers to the actions and
practices of the government.
Politicians and lawyers visited the
Van Burens' tavern to discuss politics.

polling place (POH-ling PLAYSS)
A polling place is a public building
where people go to vote. The town
of Kinderhook used Abraham Van
Buren's tavern as a polling place.

principles (PRIN-suh-puls)
Principles are people's basic beliefs,
or what they believe to be right and
true. When Van Buren stood by his
principles, he did what he felt
was right.

representative (rep-ree-ZEN-tuh-tiv)
A representative is someone who
attends a meeting, having agreed to
speak or act for others. President
John Quincy Adams wanted to send
a U.S. representative to the Panama
Congress in 1826.

republic (ree-PUB-lik)
A republic is a nation in which citizens elect representatives to their government. Texas became a republic when it won independence from Mexico.

reservations (rez-ur-VAY-shunz)
Reservations were parcels of land set aside for Native Americans by the U.S. government. Native Americans were forced off their lands and made to live on reservations.

territory (TAYR-ih-tor-ee)
A territory is land or a region, especially land that belongs to a government. Northerners did not want slavery allowed in new territories such as Florida.

treasury (TREZH-ur-ee)
A treasury manages a government's or organization's money. Van Buren set up an independent treasury to handle the country's money.

treaty (TREE-tee)
A treaty is a formal agreement made between nations. Van Buren signed treaties with Turkey and Great Britain in 1830.

truce (TROOS)
A truce is when two sides during a war agree to stop fighting for a period of time. American soldiers unfairly captured Chief Osceola during a truce.

union (YOON-yen)
A union is the joining together of two or more people or groups of people, such as states. The United States is also known as the Union.

Our PRESIDENTS

President	Birthplace	Life Span	Presidency	Political Party	First Lady
George Washington	Virginia	1732–1799	1789–1797	None	Martha Dandridge Custis Washington
John Adams	Massachusetts	1735–1826	1797–1801	Federalist	Abigail Smith Adams
Thomas Jefferson	Virginia	1743–1826	1801–1809	Democratic-Republican	widower
James Madison	Virginia	1751–1836	1809–1817	Democratic Republican	Dolley Payne Todd Madison
James Monroe	Virginia	1758–1831	1817–1825	Democratic Republican	Elizabeth Kortright Monroe
John Quincy Adams	Massachusetts	1767–1848	1825–1829	Democratic-Republican	Louisa Johnson Adams
Andrew Jackson	South Carolina	1767–1845	1829–1837	Democrat	widower
Martin Van Buren	New York	1782–1862	1837–1841	Democrat	widower
William H. Harrison	Virginia	1773–1841	1841	Whig	Anna Symmes Harrison
John Tyler	Virginia	1790–1862	1841–1845	Whig	Letitia Christian Tyler / Julia Gardiner Tyler
James K. Polk	North Carolina	1795–1849	1845–1849	Democrat	Sarah Childress Polk

Our PRESIDENTS

President	Birthplace	Life Span	Presidency	Political Party	First Lady
Zachary Taylor	Virginia	1784–1850	1849–1850	Whig	Margaret Mackall Smith Taylor
Millard Fillmore	New York	1800–1874	1850–1853	Whig	Abigail Powers Fillmore
Franklin Pierce	New Hampshire	1804–1869	1853–1857	Democrat	Jane Means Appleton Pierce
James Buchanan	Pennsylvania	1791–1868	1857–1861	Democrat	never married
Abraham Lincoln	Kentucky	1809–1865	1861–1865	Republican	Mary Todd Lincoln
Andrew Johnson	North Carolina	1808–1875	1865–1869	Democrat	Eliza McCardle Johnson
Ulysses S. Grant	Ohio	1822–1885	1869–1877	Republican	Julia Dent Grant
Rutherford B. Hayes	Ohio	1822–1893	1877–1881	Republican	Lucy Webb Hayes
James A. Garfield	Ohio	1831–1881	1881	Republican	Lucretia Rudolph Garfield
Chester A. Arthur	Vermont	1829–1886	1881–1885	Republican	widower
Grover Cleveland	New Jersey	1837–1908	1885–1889	Democrat	Frances Folsom Cleveland

	President	Birthplace	Life Span	Presidency	Political Party	First Lady
	Benjamin Harrison	Ohio	1833–1901	1889–1893	Republican	Caroline Scott Harrison
	Grover Cleveland	New Jersey	1837–1908	1893–1897	Democrat	Frances Folsom Cleveland
	William McKinley	Ohio	1843–1901	1897–1901	Republican	Ida Saxton McKinley
	Theodore Roosevelt	New York	1858–1919	1901–1909	Republican	Edith Kermit Carow Roosevelt
	William H. Taft	Ohio	1857–1930	1909–1913	Republican	Helen Herron Taft
	Woodrow Wilson	Virginia	1856–1924	1913–1921	Democrat	Ellen L. Axson Wilson Edith Bolling Galt Wilson
	Warren G. Harding	Ohio	1865–1923	1921–1923	Republican	Florence Kling De Wolfe Harding
	Calvin Coolidge	Vermont	1872–1933	1923–1929	Republican	Grace Goodhue Coolidge
	Herbert C. Hoover	Iowa	1874–1964	1929–1933	Republican	Lou Henry Hoover
	Franklin D. Roosevelt	New York	1882–1945	1933–1945	Democrat	Anna Eleanor Roosevelt Roosevelt
	Harry S. Truman	Missouri	1884–1972	1945–1953	Democrat	Elizabeth Wallace Truman

Our PRESIDENTS

President	Birthplace	Life Span	Presidency	Political Party	First Lady
Dwight D. Eisenhower	Texas	1890–1969	1953–1961	Republican	Mary "Mamie" Doud Eisenhower
John F. Kennedy	Massachusetts	1917–1963	1961–1963	Democrat	Jacqueline Bouvier Kennedy
Lyndon B. Johnson	Texas	1908–1973	1963–1969	Democrat	Claudia Alta Taylor Johnson
Richard M. Nixon	California	1913–1994	1969–1974	Republican	Thelma Catherine Ryan Nixon
Gerald Ford	Nebraska	1913–	1974–1977	Republican	Elizabeth "Betty" Bloomer Warren Ford
James Carter	Georgia	1924–	1977–1981	Democrat	Rosalynn Smith Carter
Ronald Reagan	Illinois	1911–	1981–1989	Republican	Nancy Davis Reagan
George Bush	Massachusetts	1924–	1989–1993	Republican	Barbara Pierce Bush
William Clinton	Arkansas	1946–	1993–2001	Democrat	Hillary Rodham Clinton
George W. Bush	Connecticut	1946–	2001–	Republican	Laura Welch Bush

Presidential FACTS

Qualifications

To run for president, a candidate must

- be at least 35 years old
- be a citizen who was born in the United States
- have lived in the United States for 14 years

Term of Office

A president's term of office is four years. No president can stay in office for more than two terms.

Election Date

The presidential election takes place every four years on the first Tuesday of November.

Inauguration Date

Presidents are inaugurated on January 20.

Oath of Office

I do solemnly swear I will faithfully execute the office of the President of the United States and will to the best of my ability preserve, protect, and defend the Constitution of the United States.

Write a Letter to the President

One of the best things about being a U.S. citizen is that Americans get to participate in their government. They can speak out if they feel government leaders aren't doing their jobs. They can also praise leaders who are going the extra mile. Do you have something you'd like the president to do? Should the president worry more about the environment and encourage people to recycle? Should the government spend more money on our schools? You can write a letter to the president to say how you feel!

1600 Pennsylvania Avenue
Washington, D.C. 20500

You can even send an e-mail to: president@whitehouse.gov

For Further INFORMATION

Internet Sites

Visit Martin Van Buren's Lindenwald home:
http://www.nps.gov/mava/

Find links to many Web pages and sites about Martin Van Buren:
http://www.geocities.com/CapitolHill/Lobby/5296/pres_martin_van_buren.html

Learn more about Kinderhook:
http://www.kinderhookconnection.com/history.htm

Learn more about the War of 1812:
http://www.cfcsc.dnd.ca/links/milhist/1812.html

Learn more about the Trail of Tears:
http://rosecity.net/
http://www.peaknet.net/~aardvark/

Learn more about the Aroostook War:
http://homepages.rootsweb.com/~godwin/reference/aroostook.html

Learn more about all the presidents and visit the White House:
http://www.whitehouse.gov/WH/glimpse/presidents/html/presidents.html
http://www.thepresidency.org/presinfo.htm
http://www.americanpresidents.org/

Books

Chambers, Veronica. *Amistad Rising: A Story of Freedom.* Austin, TX: Raintree/Steck-Vaughn, 1998.

Collier, Christopher, and James Lincoln. *Andrew Jackson's America.* New York: Marshall Cavendish, 1999.

Cornelissen, Cornelia. *Soft Rain: A Story of the Cherokee Trail of Tears.* New York: Delacorte Press, 1998.

Fradin, Dennis. *The New York Colony.* Chicago: Childrens Press, 1988.